This Is Not an Epiphany

Tom Branfoot

the poetry business

Published 2023 by
New Poets List
The Poetry Business
Campo House,
54 Campo Lane,
Sheffield S1 2EG

ISBN 978-1-914914-49-2
eBook ISBN 978-1-914914-50-8
Typeset by Utter
Cover image: Jason Dent on Unsplash
Printed by Biddles Books

Smith|Doorstop Books are a member of Inpress:
www.inpressbooks.co.uk

Distributed by NBN International, 1 Deltic Avenue,
Rooksley, Milton Keynes MK13 8LD

The Poetry Business gratefully acknowledges
the support of Arts Council England.

Supported by
ARTS COUNCIL
ENGLAND

Contents

'A word is elegy to what it signifies'
– Robert Hass

'Tell me something, one thing, the thing, tell me that thing'
– Claudia Rankine

'It's a long way to find peace of mind, peace of mind'
– Nick Cave

near the motorway turnoff's
midriff of noise
cheek by jowl with a graveyard
they're planning
to build a warehouse
in the flood plains
23 metres tall 317 metres long
178 metres wide   at night
the graveyard is dark silence
heaps at the stone
perimeter where the world
crouches under trees
scabbed with oakmoss
I am setting you
this very real scene
sodium streetlights
not yet replaced by LEDs
the razed grain fields
skewered with markers
what is left to soak up
rainfall to soak
up nightfall in a taxi
back home from the city
I tell the driver there is not
enough money here
and it is almost
so beautiful
I love winter and trying
to get through each day to see
the sunrise during
my predawn piss
I think we're always trying
to do the same thing
feeling safe or to perfect

the driver orders a chicken
burger to collect after drop-off
and the *Say No To Amazon*
banners are wet with glare

Return Thursday, 14th

slant cities pass in a sentence
I am fed up with all this reaching
for an approximation of beauty

was it not the brutish hour
the lights knocked out like teeth
I am no one to speak

now in the darker half of the year
bleed me like a radiator at the station
because the world is big

take these hands because the earth
is bending to a point
bleed me like a sacrifice outside

light fades in a page
The demand for love writes Barthes
in his autobiography suspended in white

sharp and tied to no subordinate clause
this is the stuff that lingers
in the stubbed October night

and I still text in longing
as if anything that came out of language
could make language tremble

Throat Clearing

it's cold today and my head aches
I'm not trying to obfuscate
I water my plants with a watering can
the government almost collapsed
how do we generate new possibilities
I'm living off tins
of miscellaneous beans
I think my friends
are growing tired of me

today is effaced by tomorrow
unless the past is here to stay
I'm not trying to obfuscate
no counsellor can prescribe time
I water my plants with the tide
laying in bed with groundbreaking
British comedy spread across my lap
one miniscule light under
a consortium of lights
this my-truth is indisputable

Portrait of a Garden

nuzzled in the crook
of your grinding teeth
I think the poem a terrarium
embracing an air plant
outside   plum blossom
bunch on trees
planted in avenues
this sticky garden
cultivated   in a single
bed   hanging in a city
uninhabitable
money leaking through
the roof when it rains
some form of water
torture   discordant
with hedgerow choir
this rented room
sclera-white   daylight
pinching at the blinds
already I'm thinking
about standing
desk exercises   fibre bars
and waiting a whole
long day to arrive   back
under the damp ceiling
cracked   by heatwave
and your light feet
tracing patterns
in plaster dust

Dread Hymn

this heart I forget it beats   wholeness
thrown and shot like a clay pigeon
at the barbed   and terraceous mouth

of the woods   grandma goes to the cathedral
for confession   so the parochial
priest does not recognise her voice

to keep it sweet with hymn
sunday morning
bodies persist in the city

churches shuttered
no saviours within a three-mile radius
of wageness   wishing to be strong

as a pharmaceutical giant
full of actual grace   not fatigued
from giving what needs to be gave

this heat I forget it sears   my possible
brightness will you come down
if I lean in to it with my animal

This Is Not an Epiphany

Let's face it. We're undone by each other. And if we're not, we're missing
something ... One does not always stay intact.
                                        – Judith Butler

from its yolky sheen and song I spotted a goldcrest
in shrubland across from the Calderdale Way
an afternoon spent catching tears on my
touchscreen   perched on a dry stone wall
heat chisels *embarrassment* as the goat
bleats *humiliation*   it began in November
as you flew south   I'm taking it like a man

                    ✳

two girls are TikTok dancing under   the shelter
of a blossom tree decorated   with just a few
cherried boughs   enough to flash in the late
sun   swaying outside the Heart and Lung
Research Centre   you hope they're only waiting
for the bus home   and not convulsing
languageless anticipating someone's results

                    ✳

there's a running joke that a regular   at the
Church Inn Uppermill always sat stooped
on a corner stool   for a sweeping view
of the valley and when they built a private
cemetery   lower in the green dale he reserved
a lot there saying it's the closest place he could
get to the end   [...] of the stout-stained bar

*

taking out the recycling   a pair of greylags
flew southwesterly   honking in the crisp
blue morning tasered by an absentee
defecting Sertraline just to trial another
capitalist palliative   waking 3 a.m.
every night until something stabilises
magpies root on the empty football field

*

Steve was my driving instructor when I was
seventeen   he said *intrusive thoughts are like
leaves floating downstream you don't have
to pick them out* he was a recovering alcoholic
and gambling addict who found God trembling
he showed me videos of the church choir parked
roadside   during my frequent panic attacks

*

[...] this is not as simple as you might think
recovering on an ailing earth   I've got too much
love left over   it won't all stay inside my body
imagine a man unstable as an atom falling apart
like radioactive decay   it began in November
such loose contours   all my layers couldn't hold
I was not multitudes   just something like water

*

I changed course turning into the gardens
of Ordsall Hall coaxed by tulip planters
and gleaming brickwork the air was warm
and still around the fragrant Tudor knot un-

12

til the groundskeeper appeared from behind
an ornamental fir and spoke to me about human
progress the lengths a nation will go to [...]

*

back at the caravan park in Ripley maybe
just me and you dad when I was 8 or 9
there was a girl Siobhán black hair blue eyes
up by the lake we fed bread to the wildfowl
until it burst into seasonal rain when I ripped
the bread bag and walked her home
wet plastic   covering her dark hair

*

cycling to Chorlton through a cyclone of cherry
blossom in the golden early evening my hands
pruned from hours soaking in the bath all day
I've been writing about regional pride which
is to say about love flourishing over time
last night I rode home by the full moon's
light as everyone grew wilder and wild

*

through the hot wind a fox screams like a boy
knifed and knifed again in the humid night
I wake feeling tumbled from the machine
all felted and bleary rousing with raw hunger
but not enough to beg I beat my fists into
my stomach because all I want is to be tender
just know I wanted kindness above all things

*

when the sun cracked like an egg on the pavement
blowing cobwebs from my limbs I flew up the
ship canal disoriented by downy gosling kneeling
to touch speared water hawthorn I don't expect
you to believe me but a dove flew out from under
the swing bridge and a man with my name spoke
softly to me [forgive me] this is not an epiphany

*

memories are luminous detached things embers
after everybody leaves I could listen to you talk
until the stars lie down like a field in lambing
season say my name because after all I am not
God's favourite why can't we carry on pretending
at least just until morning slipping between each
other like silt through water our mouths open

Parenthesis

swifts circumflex the sky   dull as the underside

of tinfoil   the cleanness of GM fruit

I research the day we met as an astronomical event

packed to the flanks   with onyx and Citalopram

it was the 28th day of summer

mothlike and sweet   as if everything is powered

by contrast   if time worked for us

this gift would be a barrel of Brent crude oil

heart-shaped nights in the Midland Hotel

not even stunned   but an absence of violence

instead I refuse to pay rent   until they plaster

my asymmetric wounds

In Every House Nobody Sleeps

nocturnal out here in wild escape
the gauzy texture of extreme heat
Walthamstow and Leyton
beyond arguments sheltered
by hedgerows swallowing benches
we know it's light pollution
smouldering the East London fresco
but think this stifling haze
an aureole draped over
commons scorched but open
it's just a bit of debris you say
edging closer to the breathing mass
saint to an angel   equal parts
trepidation and awe knowing
to touch a thing is to ruffle its world
stippled as a skyline in your torch
pin-dropped in this strip
not jammed against blades
or mauled unmendably
but snuffling still touched
by light before commuting
into the undergrowth we whis-
per *I love you small companion*
burnt   by business as usual

Lodgings

if you knew it would happen then why
did you let it   *on my tod* meaning
death meaning ivy meaning own
rows of poplars in a lawned
golf course do nothing   the hedge
fund managers do nothing
knowing property is the square root of rain
if you knew entropy   would you reproduce
or that green on maps wasn't accessible
would you even move
I am a carpark crowded with carsized aches
an old elevator with wrought
iron doors creaking with the weight
of my civil disobedience   bladder
like a cloud   fuck this I want a house
in the country pebbledashed with stars

By Contrast My Alcove

is teeming
with microplastics
chewing on hops
eyes hooded like monks
brewing a recipe
that never alters
in a structure
that never alters
like lead
sickly to lick
with a peasant tongue
a crone tongue
upright as an icon
everything has been
said about time
except that it unfurls
like spores of lead
under a sycamore
older than serfdom
I wonder what monks
do for fun
the grass looks fake
in the almshouse
I want to chew
on something gross
to digest power
into bitesize chunks
and lock myself
away for as long

as it takes to drive
reparations
down the M1
tell me something
fun now
something intractable

Owling

in the black soup of lampless country   you goggle the window

for nightbirds   while I stare forward searching for nothing

in the mud and rain rorschach   the fragile grit

of a decommissioned child   my libido siphoned

at the crossroads   tomorrow there will be a solar storm

disorienting animals   and trains will be cancelled

by an atmospheric wind   unvoyaging on the hourly bus

seats occupied by diminutive hopes   we are running

out of air in the archives of winter   there are no owls

only exhausted snowdrops   maybe it's the brooding

in my heartburn   which attunes me to the earth

below the thin soles   of these dead man's shoes

the gale in your breath   turbulent with dissatisfaction

uproots hairs on my neck   your feral engine turning over

practising happiness   I want you in a small miserable way

Boxcutter

I never wanted to be a saint
not that I could
be free from wreck
& anyway
I have work tomorrow
what a state I feel
on the 149
proximate to midnight
sandpaper throat
waning eyes
my body needs rest
& lime blossom tea
not fasting or flagellation
discarded bones
on the pavement

---

next door's dog has died   they're having
a funeral in the commons burying
him under a douglas fir   dog walkers
walk past   hurriedly clutching
a seven-headed leash   the mulberry
is hollow to the fruit
outside the lodge   someone plays
flute for the elderly if only my flatmate
played flute for the elderly   though
it's probably voluntary   read doable
for those with rich parents   read hunger
for those without
my eyes see sheets of unreal rain

———————————

no one wanted to talk
while I was having a piss
the world ends every day
I lose you
lose grip on a synthesis
here
I should apply humour
like a boxcutter
I just want my flatmate
to get a job
I just want to talk
with my flatmate while
having a piss
this is not the joke
here is the joke
at night I wrap myself
in tattered anthems
because it's cold
when the sun
hides
stateless with guilt

———————————

finding it hard to find time
toggled myself in the fear-duffel
real hate myself hours
the payday list vascular
I am an organic sanctuary
a business calendar
with modernist design principles

the ghost tree is in flower
on my lunch break I haunt it

———————————

making a connection home
I walk down Keats Grove
though I dwell in uncertainty
I was never
infected by his verse
parakeets scream
over walnut trees
& Grand Designs houses
reaching
South End Road
discharged from the green
& pleasant into pre
carious blossom
if this were an aphorism
I would see it now
all the subtle romance
but it does nothing for me
the fenced-off grounds
violence in the grove
I walk into the corner
shop top up my Oyster
and bloom in the sunset
bloom in the station
bloom on the train

Notes to the Poems

Epigraphs are from: 'Meditation at Lagunitas' by Robert Hass, in the collection *Praise* (1979, HarperCollins); 'Hollywood' by Nick Cave & The Bad Seeds from the album *Ghosteen* (2019, Bad Seeds Ltd) and Just Us by Claudia Rankine (2020, Penguin).

Return Thursday, 14th
The italicised text is from *Roland Barthes* by Roland Barthes trans. Richard Howard (1996, Papermac).

Throat Clearing
Inspiration for the final three lines comes from Georges Didi-Huberman's *Survival of the Fireflies* trans. Lia Swope Mitchell (2018, Minnesota University Press), kindly introduced to me by Cameron Etherton in the Cittie of Yorke, Holborn.

Portrait of a Garden
Shortlisted for The Bridport Prize for Poetry 2022 and dedicated to Jasmine Boston.

Dread Hymn
was published in bath magg, my gratitude to the editors.

This Is Not an Epiphany
Epigraph taken from Judith Butler's *Precarious Life: The Powers of Mourning and Violence* (2006, Verso Books).

In Every House Nobody Sleeps
This poem is dedicated to David Dobson, with whom I shared this encounter. Lines 18-20 rework those in 'The Mower' by Philip Larkin, from *Collected Poems* (Faber & Faber, 1988).

By Contrast My Alcove
Published in *Lessons in Gravity: Poems from Museum of the Home*
(2022), this poem was written between March and July in workshops
led by Anthony Anaxagorou.